A HATFUL OF DRAGONS

And More Than 13.8 Billion Other Funny Poems

VIKRAM MADAN

HarperCollins*Children's Books*

WORDSONG
AN IMPRINT OF BOYDS MILLS & KANE
New York

To my parents, Anita and Om, for everything

First published in India in 2022 by HarperCollins Children's Books
An imprint of HarperCollins *Publishers*
Building No 10, Tower A, 4th Floor, DLF Cyber City, Phase II,
Gurugram – 122002
www.harpercollins.co.in

Published by arrangement with Wordsong, an imprint of Boyds Mills & Kane,
a division of Astra Publishing House
wordsongpoetry.com

P-ISBN: 978-93-5629-485-1
E-ISBN: 978-93-5629-486-8

Design by Barbara Grzeslo
The text is set in Futura Bold.
The titles are set in Futura Medium.
The cover illustration was created with ink
and watercolors. Other illustrations were
hand-drawn on a tablet computer.
Printed at Nutech Print Services - India

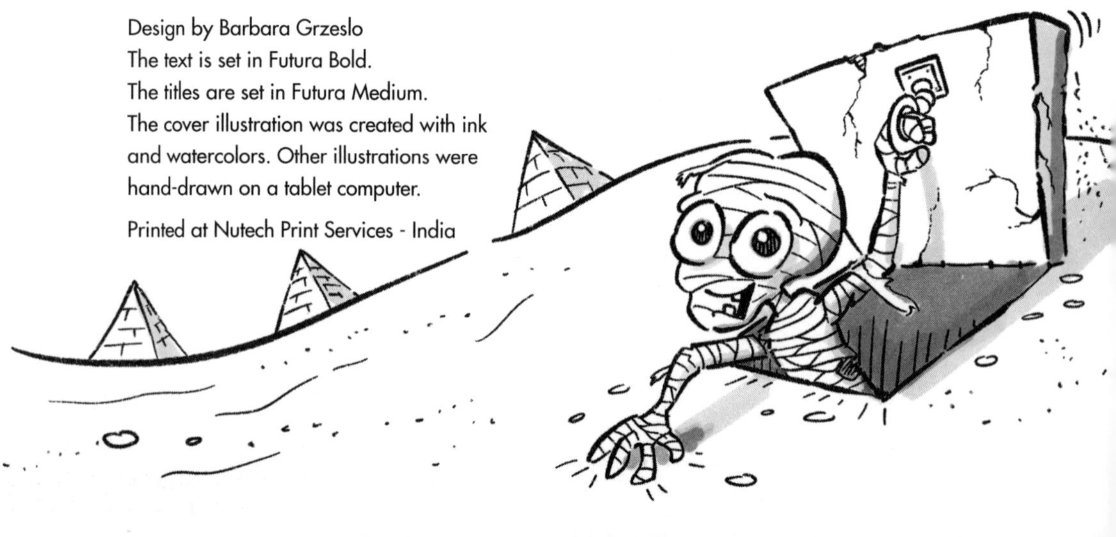

Contents

THE PANDA AND THE PANGOLIN

**The Panda and the Pangolin
Between them have a mandolin,
A clarinet, a violin,
A drum made from some beaten tin.**

**They gather in the Panda's den.
They tune their instruments, and then
They jam from two o'clock till ten,
Take one short break, and start again.**

**And all is good, except, you see,
They lack all sense of harmony.
Each note they blare—they know just three—
Sounds like an irate honeybee.**

And to their neighbor's deep dismay,
Incessantly, all night and day,
With gusto, passion, and sashay,
They orchestrate a shrill soiree.

With just three notes they make a din,
With clarinet, with violin,
With drum of tin, with mandolin,
That Panda and that Pangolin.

Meanwhile next door . . .

THE NEIGHBOR'S DISMAY

Oh . . . it's grating, irritating, and it's getting on my nerves.
This is worse than any torment that my dear old soul deserves.
All the music that my neighbors play is arduous to bear—
A dissonant cacophony from an overenthused pair.
Now I'm sure that if I stay here I shall fly into a rage
So I'm packing up my bags and moving to some other page!

TAXI
TAXI

SALE
BUY NOW
CLICK
DELIVERY
screech!
YAY!!!
RUSH
FRAGILE

BAMBOOZLED

I . . . am . . . fuming, I . . . am . . . furious,
I . . . am angry—hopping mad!
I've been cheated. I've been swindled.
I've been bamboozled and had.

I was told the eggs I bought would
Hatch me DRAGONS by the scores,
But these eggs are clearly faulty . . .

. . . They're just hatching DINOSAURS!

THE HAUNTING

A ghost is floating by the door.
It's trying hard to scare me.
Its chains are spread across the floor.
I think it's trying to snare me.

It's flickering with horrid howls
And ill-portending grumpy growls.
It's smoldering with sullen scowls
As if this should despair me.

A ghost is floating in my room.
It's haunting me with vigor.
I might have felt some sense of doom . . .

. . . If only it were bigger.

THE FLIPPY, FLOPPY FLAPPERS

Oh, those flippy, floppy flappers are
A fairly flouncy lot
As they bound with manic energy
From spot to spot to spot.

They keep leaping lapping looping as
They flop and flip and flap.
They can barely bear to idle and
They rarely nab a nap.

They go sproinging, they go boinging,
Leaving chaos in their wake.
You can always sense them coming
Like an imminent earthquake.

Oh, those flippy, floppy flappers are
A breezy, bouncy bunch,
And I very much regret that we . . .

. . . Invited them to lunch.

THE HELPFUL PET

We are sitting in a wrangle
Of a knotty, twelve-limb tangle—
Where we're starting, where we're ending
Is a puzzle through and through.

I no longer think it's clever
When you're late for school as ever
To invite your octopus to
Tie the laces on your shoe.

PRICKLY LOT

**Dragons? They're a prickly lot!
Cranky, crabby, grouchy, hot!
Sulky, surly, sullen, cross!
Oversteeped in upset-sauce!**

**Volcanic and volatile,
Not one trace of laugh or smile.
You might wonder, "Why such ire?"
Here's the answer: "Dragon Fire!"**

**That inferno in their maw
Has a fundamental flaw—
Everything they try to eat
Scorches in their fiery heat!**

Salty, spicy, tangy, sweet,
Veggie, fruit, or slab of meat—
Every morsel, nibble, shard
Ends up blistered, burned, and charred.

All their munchies taste like ash!
How that makes them fume and thrash,
Makes them snappy, huffy, hot.
Dragons—they're a prickly lot!

13,841,287,201* NONSENSE POEMS IN ONE!

Fill in the numbered blank with your choice from the corresponding numbered list to create YOUR VERY OWN one-of-a-kind nonsense poem.

I met a ____(1)______ sitting by the __(2)_____.
She said, "___________(3)____________
Can you spare ____(4)____ for _______(5)_____?
The _____(6)_____ conspiring against my reign!"

I gave her _____(7)____ and _____(8)_____.
She said, "_____(9)__________"
She _____(10)______ and __________(11)____–
Then ___(12)____ away without waving goodbye.

** Each blank has 7 choices. Fill in 1 blank 7 different ways and you can have 7 different poems. Fill in 2 blanks with 7 different choices each and you can create 7 times 7 = 49 different poems. With 12 blanks offering 7 choices each, you can create 7 x 7 x 7 x 7 x 7 x 7 x 7 x 7 x 7 x 7 x 7 x 7 = 13,841,287,201 possible poems. Don't believe me? Ask a math teacher!*

(1)
rabbit
panda
werewolf
robot
teacher
baby
monster

(2)
junkyard
spaceship
playground
palace
ocean
bookstore
dump truck

(3)
Four oysters live inside my drain.
Do zombies hunger for my brain?
I left my homework on the train.
I love to chew on sugarcane.
Can we travel by paper plane?
A ghost once snared me with a chain.
Does thinking cause a lot of strain?

(4)
a pangolin
your pet pixie
chili peppers
your left stocking
day-old coffee
six syllables
twenty marbles

(5)
a ballet
my uncles
three weekends
a cat race
a lost cause
our supper
these dragons

(6)
smell is
slobs are
cold is
hats are
night is
germs are
fish are

(7)
fifty kittens
three wet puppies
two stale bagels
forty comics
my report card
all my cousins
fries and haggis

(8)
a flu shot
an onion
the mayor
two old socks
two tubas
my aunt Flo
a noodle

(9)
I'm great at making ogres cry.
My frenemy is a housefly.
Let's waltz on top of this bonsai.
Can I please mail you to Shanghai?
My hamster moonlights as a spy.
The smell of cabbage makes me sigh.
Let's snack upon my yellow tie.

(10)
kissed my buttered toast
licked my emu eggs
picked my pocket clean
gave me half a grape
ruffled my toupee
hugged my best kazoo
curdled all the milk

(11)
did some yoga
yodeled, "Yee-haw"
whistled poorly
stole my pink hat
sang a ballad
hacked my website
scored a touchdown

(12)
twirled
skulked
flew
hiked
pranced
inched
jumped

OUR FAVORITE UNCLE

So we got ourselves an Uncle from the corner Uncle Store.
He's an enterprising Uncle with a moustache and a snore.
He comes loaded with six magic tricks (there's room for dozens more!)
His infectious laugh is thunderous, just like a lion's roar.
When we come back home from school, we find him waiting by the door.
How he makes us hoot and giggle till we're tickled to our core.
He knows fifty thousand stories, not a single one a bore.
All his pockets always overflow with sweets and treats galore.
If we climb onto his back, he'll gladly crawl on all his fours.
He can juggle; he can whistle; he will even do our chores!

And if ever he gets overwhelmed, this Uncle we adore . . .

. . . That's when he gets his *OWN* Uncles from the corner Uncle Store!

PERMANENT GUESTS

Ten aliens and a garden gnome
Have turned my shoe into their home.
They came this morning carrying sacks
And boxes full of knicks and knacks.
They sawed out windows and a door
And laid down carpets on the floor.
They sprayed the inside pink, with stripes,
And then, for plumbing, added pipes.
All done, they took a break for tea
Ten aliens and their one gnomie.
I've scrutinized their work all day.
It looks like they are here to stay.
And I don't mind a thing they do . . .

. . . Except my foot's
still in my shoe.

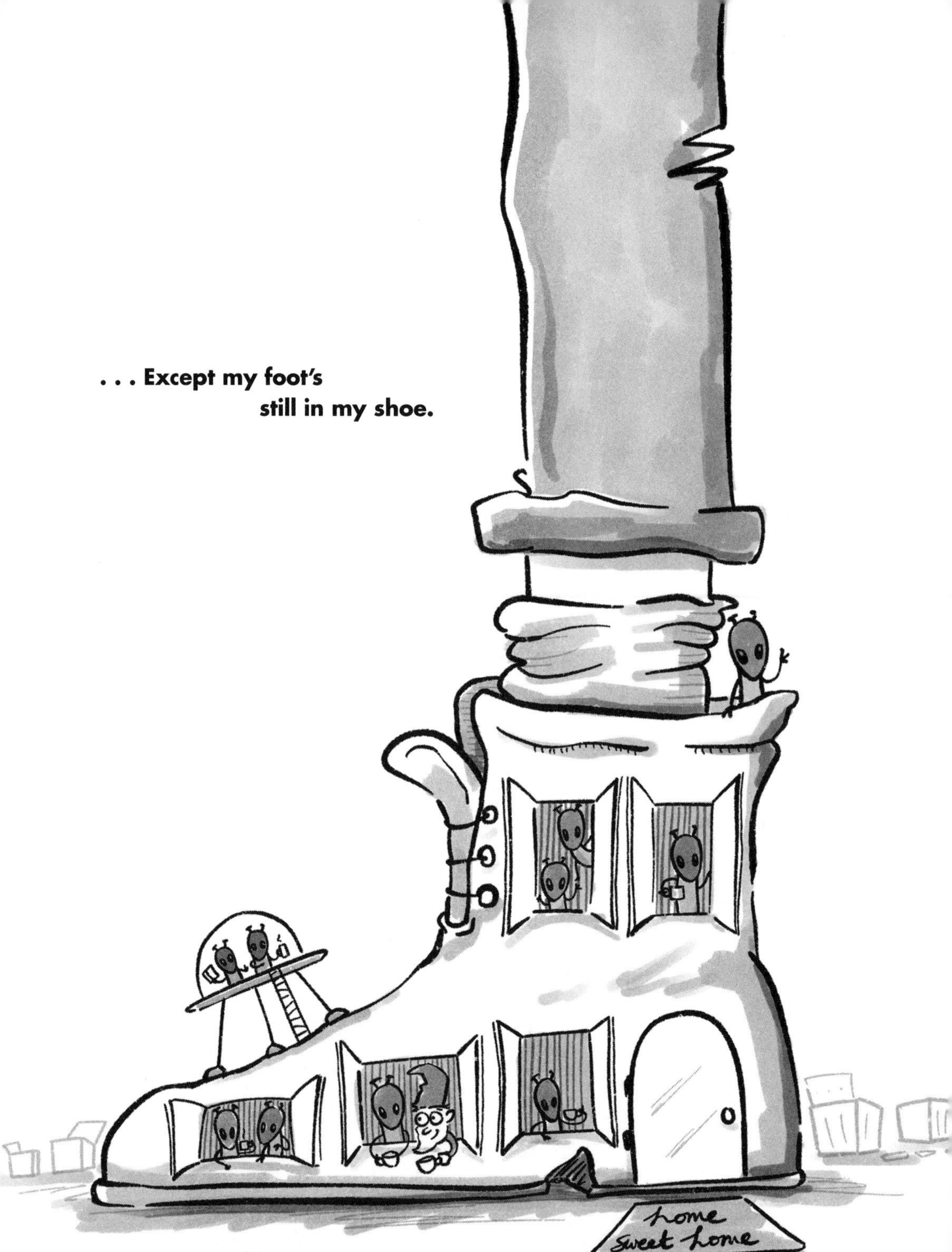

TAXI CRAB

A crabber and a crabby crab
Sat eating cabbage in a cab
When suddenly the crabber grabbed
The cabbage from the crabby crab,
Which made the crab more crabby still—
He snipped and snapped his claws until
The cabbie turned around to blab,
"No crabbiness inside my cab!
No crabbiness! No grabbiness!
No snipping-snapping jabbiness!
If you two do not curb your rage,
I'll dump you on the seventh page!"

THERE'S A DRAGON IN MY WAGON

There's a dragon in my wagon
Plunking, plonking his guitar.
He's been making merry music
All the way from Zanzibar.

While his playing is discordant
And his rhythm unrefined
And his vocals boom and thunder—
These are not the things I mind.

What has kindled my annoyance,
Riling, roiling me so long,
Is this dragon in my wagon
Seems to only know one song.

YUM-YUM FOOD

The Dragon's Ditty

(Sing to the tune of "Jingle Bells")

(Verse)

I dream of yum-yum food
That's salty, sour, and sweet.
I dream of spicy food.
I dream of yum-yum treats.

I dream that I can taste
Each morsel, nibble, shard.
I dream that all my yum-yum food
Won't always be so charred.
(Repeat from the beginning, endlessly)

LOUDER

**LOUDER than a dragon singing
LOUDER than Niagara Falls
LOUDER than an alley full of
Cats engaged in caterwauls.**

**LOUDER than a pre-K recess
LOUDER than a bandits' brawl
LOUDER than ten puppies yapping
At a vacuum cleaner's drawl.**

**LOUDER than an airplane's engine
LOUDER than a summer squall . . .**

. . . Is the CRACKLE of my chip bag
At the movies in the mall!

BROUHAHA

A Cracked-Concrete Poem

My poem wasn't tight—a word slipped out and fell.
It landed on the below and ruptured that as well.
What opus could the weight of words with such impact?
My rhymes were rickety, but now my structure's cracked!
The meter flailed, rhythm quailed, the syllables played dead.
Concurrent with brouhaha, the verses cursed and fled.
More words fell as lines caved in from inconsistent stress.
If there's still left in here, it's underneath this mess.

TU-BAA-BAA

Oom-PAH, Oom-PAH, Oom-PAH-PAH—
Hear us play the Tu-BAA-BAA.
We *BLAARP*, we *PAARP*, we BLOW-BLOW-BLOW.
We play it deep and low-low-low.
We play it fast and slow-slow-slow.
We polka as we go-go-go—
Pol-KAA, Pol-KAA, Pol-KAA-KAA-KAA.
We hope you'll *OOOH* and *AAH-AAH-AAH*
And for one dollar, two, or four . . .

We promise we will play no more!

UNRULY BUNCH

The oysters are feeling so boisterous tonight
They're acting unruly and wild.
They're whooping and cheering
Reveling and jeering
(Though outwardly they still look mild).

The oysters are rowdy and noisy tonight.
They're making an anarchic scene.
The reef's getting frantic
About their rude antics
(Though outwardly they look serene).

The oysters are roistering full swing tonight.
The seabed's their big party zone.
And if you cannot tell
What goes on in their shell
Don't worry, for you're not alone.

THE POUCH

**There goes a kangaroo,
Dexterous and strong
Endlessly, wendlessly,
Hopping along**

**And deep in her pouch,
Where no one can see,
Is a cute little joey . . .**

. . . And stuck little me.

ITTY BITTY MONSTROSITIES

Mummy wrapped in
Hoary cloths—
Scrumptious feast for
Hungry moths.

SLOBBERLY SLOBS

We're Slobberly Slobs! We're Slobberly Slobs!
We're dirty! We're trashy! We litter by gobs!
We're loud and we're crude!
Expressively rude!
We look like a rabble of raggedy blobs!

We're Slobberly Slobs! We're Slobberly Slobs!
If things are too tidy, we snivel and sob.
Hygienic or clean?
We must intervene!
The greater the clutter, the more our hearts throb!

We're Slobberly Slobs!

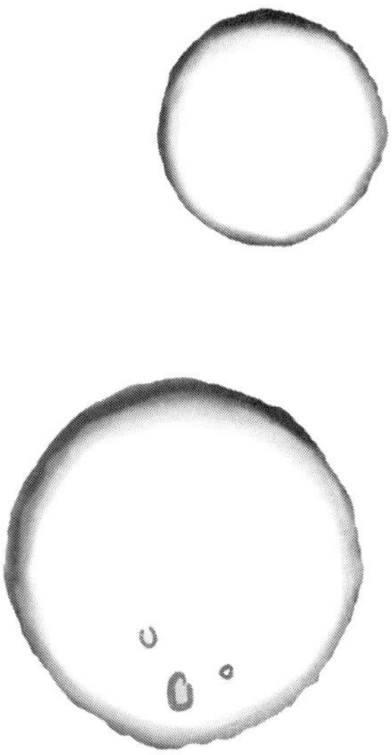

THE NEIGHBOR'S RANT

I left my prior page in rage
Because of endless, irksome din.
At long, at last I found this page—
A peaceful place to shelter in.

A wall with holes? That seemed so quaint.
But yet again I have to dash!
For through these holes, with no restraint,
Someone keeps dumping all their trash!

A HATFUL OF DRAGONS

A hatful of diamonds? Will make you feel rich!
A hatful of pepper? Will make your nose itch!
A hatful of dragons? ???
HATFUL
DRAGONS
A hatful of barbers? Could shave your head bald!
A hatful of babies? Will leave you well crawled!
A hatful of dragons? ???
HATFUL
DRAGONS
A hatful of monsters? Might give you a fright!
A hatful of phantoms? Will haunt you all night!
A hatful of dragons? ???
DRAGONS

A hatful of aunties?
Will pinch both your cheeks!
A hatful of garlic?
Will pungently reek!
A hatful of dragons?
???
DRAGONS
A hatful of oysters?
Will riotously jeer!
A hatful of monkeys?
Might swing from your ears!
A hatful of dragons?
???
A hatful of tubas?
You'll start your own band!
A hatful of sandstorms?
That's way too much sand!
A hatful of dragons?
???

With a hatful
of dragons—
you might rule
this land!

DUEL WITH A MOSQUITO

**Oh, no! Oh, no!
That mosquito!
It bit my knee
And chomped my toe.**

**I try my best
To make it go
But it comes back
And whines, "Hello!"**

**I swing, I swat
I thwack, I throw
I pummel, punch
And land a blow.**

**But then I find,
Much to my woe
This mosquito . . .**

. . . Knows tae kwon do!

FIFTY UKELELES

I bought fifty ukuleles
At the local flea bazaar
For I wanna, wanna, wanna
Be a ukulele star.

I bought fifty ukuleles
So that I can learn to strum
Like a ukulele master
With a ukulele thumb.

I bought fifty ukuleles
So no matter where I go
I can practice, practice daily
For my ukulele show.

I bought fifty ukuleles
And they barely cost a thing.
Why, oh why, did I not notice
That not one of them has strings?

TIME MACHINE

Come step right up and take a spin
Inside my nifty time machine.
I built it from recyclables—
It's eco-friendly, extra-green.

How does it work? You enter now,
And exit at a future time.
Come step right up and take a spin.
The ticket only costs a dime!

OK! I'LL TRY IT!
IN YOU GO!
WOW! DID YOU INVENT TIME TRAVEL?
SLAM!
WHO SAID ANYTHING ABOUT TIME TRAVEL?!?
ALL I SAID WAS YOU GO IN NOW AND COME OUT IN THE FUTURE.
WHEN IN THE FUTURE?
GENUINE TIME MACHINE
RIGHT AFTER I GET SOME CANDY WITH MY DIMES!
COMING?
GENUINE TIME MACHINE
GENUINE TIME MACHINE
HEY! LET ME OUT OF HERE!
BANG! BANG!

THE THIN TWIN'S TIN

A Twingue Twister

There was a twin
who had a twin
And his twin's twin
had one thin tin—
A thing of tin
as thick (or thin)
As tin things tend to be.

One twin was thinner
than his kin.
The thin twin's twin
had no thin tin.
The thin twin's tin
had no tin twin—
No twin tin thing had he.

The thin twin's twin's
twin's twin's twin's twin
The tinless twin
who had nothin'
The tinless twin
who was less thin—
That less-thin twin? It's me!

And though I'm not
the twin who's thin
This thick-thin thing
makes my head spin.
I'm glad I only
have one twin
And not five, four, or three!

ROLLER COASTER

This roller coaster's AWESOME
And FIFTY kinds of cool!
Its heights are death-defying!
Its swoops will make you drool!

Its loops will make you loopy!
Its swirls will make you shriek!
The wind will blow your hair off as
You whiz from peak to peak!

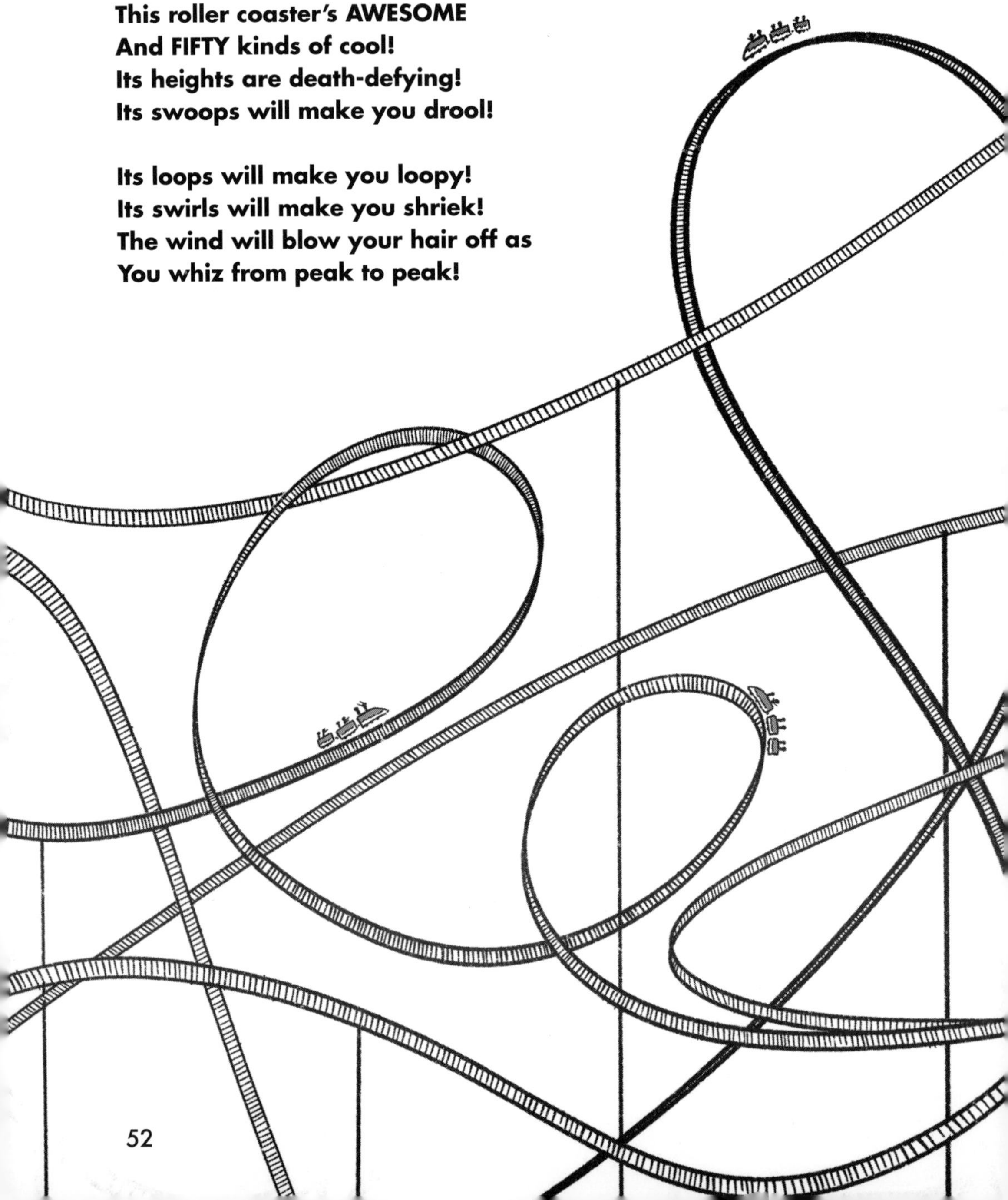

The treasures in your pockets
Will slip out one by one!
This roller coaster's awesome
And *maybe* lots of fun . . .
But . . .
I'm getting somewhat nervous
And anxious in my heart.
Please let me, let me, let me
Get off before it starts!

Use This Key To Read The Next Poem

PLATYPUS

ECHIDNA

BILBY

BAT

WOMBAT

EMU

WALLAROO

KOALA

RAT

KANGAROO

NUMBAT

POTOROO

COCKATOO

AUSTRALIAN ANIMAL CHANT

THE BAND-AID AND THE CHEWING GUM

Said Band-Aid, "My dear Chewing Gum,
I'm feeling sad and stuck.
We've both been used and cast away,
Abandoned to this muck.
This is the end, my sticky friend—
I fear we're out of luck!"

Said Chewing Gum, "O Band-Aid, dear,
Yes, fate might make us cry,
But looking up, I see bright hope
In endless open sky—
For when you're down, there's nowhere left
To go but up, and high!"

"O Chewing Gum," Band-Aid replied,
"How wise you are, my friend!
I feel the glue lift from my eyes—
You're right, it's not the end.
If only we could leave this muck
I'm sure our luck will mend!"

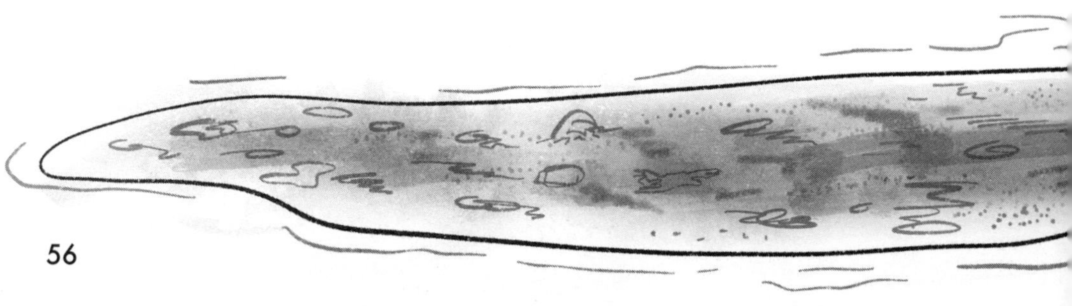

"You must have faith," said Chewing Gum,
"I have a plan in mind."
And so they waited patiently,
Till one day fate was kind
And sent to them the means by which
To leave the bog behind.

Plucked from the muck, they soared and swooped
From here to Timbuktu.
They traveled far and wide and soon
Their every dream came true
As happy as two things could be
Stuck under my left shoe.

AAAH! PEACE AND QUiET AT LAST!

READY? ONE, TWO, THREE...
PUT MONEY HERE

HELLO!
CAN WE
JOiN YOU?

PSSSSSSSTTTT!!!

My name's Professor Dobbleydook,
Inventor of the Page Machine,
Which lets me travel through this book
To spy on any page or scene.

When traveling through space and rhyme
I like to go incognito.
Should you spot me some page, sometime
I hope you'll pause to say hello!

CHiPS
~HATFUL~
~HATFUL~

meaning
the
very
always
withstand
line
this
mute